THE TOWN BELOW THE GROUND

THE TOWN BELOW THE GROUND

EDINBURGH'S LEGENDARY UNDERGROUND CITY

JAN-ANDREW HENDERSON

MAINSTREAM
PUBLISHING

EDINBURGH AND LONDON

This edition, 2008

First published in 1999 by
MAINSTREAM PUBLISHING COMPANY
(EDINBURGH) LTD
7 Albany Street Edinburgh EH1 3UG

ISBN 9781840182316

Reprinted 1999, 2000, 2001, 2002, 2003, 2004, 2007

A catalogue record for this book is available from the
British Library

Typeset in Garamond

Printed and bound in Great Britain by
CPI Cox and Wyman, Reading, RG1 8EX

Contents

Introduction

Some people believe there is a city under the pavements of Edinburgh; a dark, mysterious, forgotten place. They say it is a metropolis – that miles of streets and houses exist down there – banished forever from the light. Others claim there is no underground city – that the town below the ground isn't real. It is a fairy-tale, no more than a legend. The truth, in fact, is somewhere in-between.

There is an underground city; it is a near-mythical place, but it does exist. And you can find it – if you know where to look.

Edinburgh is an impressive city – the towering spires and ancient buildings of the Old Town are a constant feast for the eye. With so much beauty and history on display it does not occur to many visitors that there might be anything of great interest under their feet. The same is true of Edinburgh's own inhabitants – residents often have only a vague historical knowledge of the town where they live. Ask a cross-section of the local population about the underground city and you will get an astonishing array of answers. In Edinburgh's case, however, the citizens have good reason for their lack of information as throughout its history the city has been plagued by pillaging invaders and devastating fires and this has destroyed many records and archives.

There is no doubt that the legend of an underground city has been part of Edinburgh lore as long as anyone can remember. I first heard of it as a student at Edinburgh University but, like so many living in the city, I had no idea what it was or even if it really existed. The same was true of everyone I asked. I talked to retired citizens who had spent their entire lives in Edinburgh. Many had been told stories of a city below the streets when they were children, but they were still unsure where or in what form that city actually was. The intrigue surrounding this mythical place had far greater scope than I imagined. When I first met my wife, I was astonished to find that she too had heard of an underground city in Edinburgh – even though she was born and brought up in Texas. Her father had told her about the legend. He, in turn, had heard of the existence of a town below the ground on a visit to Edinburgh in the 1950s.

This book is the first to explore the idea that there was a city under the streets of Scotland's capital. It explores what the underground city actually was, how it came about and where it can still be found. It also relates the stories that have made this strange, hidden world a place of infamy. These tales stretch across the centuries – from the city's founding to the present day. They include fables, urban legends and some pretty astonishing facts. Where possible I have tried to separate truth from invention, but the truth, of course, has turned out to be far stranger.

PART ONE

*The History
and the Location*

Ancient History

There has been some sort of settlement on the site of Edinburgh since prehistoric times – and it is not hard to see why. Anyone who has witnessed the neck-straining splendour of Edinburgh Castle will testify that it is a superb defensive position.

Castle Rock was the focal point of Old Edinburgh and has been the site of some sort of fortress since Roman times. The first recorded settlers, around 2,000 years ago, were a tribe called the Vottadini (a Roman name – they were also called the Gododdin) who lived on the ridge running down from Castle Rock – the area now known as the Royal Mile or High Street. This ridge towered over the surrounding meadows and was easy to defend which made it an ideal spot for the settlement to grow.

The rock and ridge formation that provided a

Detail of plan of Edinburgh by James Gordon of
Rothiemay in 1647, showing the crowded nature of
housing in the High Street (Edinburgh City Museums)

haven for the first settlers is a geological structure called a crag and tail. The crag is a volcanic branch, one of the outlet valves for the extinct volcano that formed Arthur's Seat. During the last Ice Age the basalt strata that formed Castle Rock was too hard to be eroded by advancing glaciers. A ridge of much softer sandstone (the 'tail') also survived as it was shielded from the ice by the basalt crag. Once a fort was established on the towering crag, houses could then be safely built on the tail as any attacker would have an uphill struggle to overrun the settlement. If any invaders had succeeded in taking the ridge then the defenders simply retreated to the fort and continued the fight.

But this high ridge of soft sandstone also gave Edinburgh a unique quality that other cities simply did not have; one that was not considered by its citizens at first: you could dig into it and have an underground city.

The First Underground City
– The Lands

In the early days of the city's evolution there was no need for anyone to live underground. A combination of natural hardship, English invasions and the occasional deadly pestilence kept the population to an acceptable level and there was plenty of room for everyone. Houses spread eastwards from the castle in two leisurely rows and, at the back of these dwellings, steep inclines plunged down to the pastures in the north and south. These slopes were divided into sections called 'tenements' or 'enclosures' – a word later shortened to 'close'. The enclosures were carefully tended and provided the settlement with land for growing crops and grass for common grazing. In later times, however, this pastoral idyll would completely disappear – and the

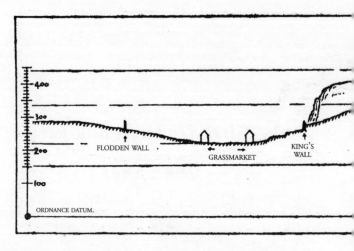

Cross-section through the Grassmarket and Castle Hill looking west, showing the King's Wall and Flodden Wall

term 'close' would take on a far more unpleasant connotation.

At this stage, the High Street bore no resemblance to the monstrosity that it would become and, as yet, none of the thatched houses even reached twenty feet high. But years passed and the town began to increase in size and importance. Early in the twelfth century the first signs that Edinburgh was a royal city are found and, despite the hardships of medieval times, the population continued to grow. It was still a pleasant place to live apparently and Froissart, visiting in 1384, called Edinburgh the 'Paris of Scotland'.

In 1450 the Scottish and English armies clashed at the Battle of Sark and, for a change, the Scots won.

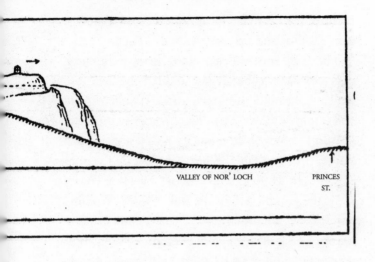

VALLEY OF NOR' LOCH   PRINCES
ST.

In case this victory goaded the enemy into yet another invasion it was decided to build a defensive wall around the city as it was felt that Edinburgh was too close to the English border for comfort. James II of Scotland granted a petition to the city burghers to begin construction. By this charter they were free to:

> fosse, bulwark, wall, tour, turate and
> otherwise strengthen the burgh, but only in
> what manner of wise or degre that beis maist
> spectefulle to the Provost of Edinburgh.

The city wall ran from the foot of Castle Rock, up the slope, and encompassed the upper part of the Royal Mile. As an extra defence the north pastures (which today form Princes Street Gardens) were flooded and became the North Loch.

The loch and wall may have made Edinburgh easier to defend, but it also limited the area into which a steadily rising population could expand and, suddenly, overcrowding became a problem. Protocol books, written by city notaries, show that building control in the old days was fairly non-existent. In 1500 Protocol books by John Fowler show the ground within the wall rapidly becoming covered by tall buildings. These buildings were known as 'lands' (now more commonly known as tenements) and grew to an average of ten or even eleven storeys. One block in Parliament Square reached the dizzy height of fourteen storeys.

Since space was at a premium, advantage was also taken of the soft sandstone. As the buildings of Old Edinburgh were erected higher and higher, the foundations became deeper and countless cellars were created. The steep slopes on either side of the High Street meant that these foundations and cellars didn't necessarily have to be excavated from above – builders could dig sideways into the ridge, allowing underground levels to be built at a depth that would not have been possible in any other location. This geographically defiant creation really was an unusual base on which to build a city. In many ways, the foundations of the tenements resembled a rabbit warren, and the cellars were more like caves slotted into the hillside. Though open at one end, the further into the hillside they went, the further under the main buildings they were. And, because of the steepness of the sides of the crag and tail, levels of cellars could be built, one above the other. But though these excavations were sideways rather than straight down, they were just as dark, wet and cold. This was the start of the underground city.

In 1513, James IV of the House of Stuart was on the throne, and was widely considered to be one of the greatest kings Scotland had ever had. He was charming and intelligent, and under his rule the country looked set to flourish at last – but, like so many of the Stuart kings, he threw it all away. To help the French in yet another cross-Channel war he invaded England, and the Scots and English armies met at Flodden. It was a pointless battle fought for an ungrateful ally and it became Scotland's greatest military disaster.

James had sent his best artillerymen to help France. The army marched south where it met the Duke of Surrey's second-string army. Though James had the better defensive position and larger cannon, Surrey had artillerymen who actually knew what they were doing. The ensuing bombardment destroyed James's guns, forcing the Scots to leave their position and attack.

At four o'clock the Scottish spearmen charged down the hill, having taken off their shoes to get a better grip on the slippery ground. They were armed with the traditional pike – a fifteen-foot spear – but the English had a new weapon, the halberd. The halberd was a combination of spear and axe and was far more manoeuvrable than the long pike. It could also be used to chop down as well as thrust forward. One chop with a halberd and the Scots found their fifteen-foot pikes were seven-foot pikes then four-foot pikes. Eventually they were fighting with toothpicks. Rank after rank of Scots was annihilated. In the meantime, James IV, leading the centre battalion, actually fought through the English soldiers to within a spear's length of Surrey before he was killed.

James was so loved that many Scots refused to acknowledge his death, preferring to believe that he had survived and journeyed to Jerusalem.

The death of King James caused total panic in Edinburgh. Since almost the entire Scots army was wiped out, nobody was left alive to defend the city from counter-invasion. And as weaponry – especially cannons – had greatly improved, the old walls were no longer considered adequate for keeping the English army at bay. The inhabitants of the Cowgate – then a new and aristocratic suburb – were particularly horrified since they were completely outside the city's defences.

While the funeral bells tolled in the background,

the people of Edinburgh formed volunteer groups and began to build another, larger, defensive wall around their city. Meanwhile, twenty-four of the town's strongest men were recruited to keep watch and alert the builders to any approaching force. This watch eventually became the famous Edinburgh 'Old Town Guard'. The rest of the population toiled on, their swords lying within arm's reach, and – in an astonishingly short space of time – the whole city, including the Cowgate, was enclosed.

The Flodden Wall was a far more impressive structure than its predecessor of 1450. It measured twenty-three feet in height and its walls were five-feet thick. It had gates, parapets and towers studded with loopholes and embrasures. The wall started at the castle and went south to the foot of the Grassmarket. Then it ascended the Vennel as far as Lauriston and turned north to what is now Bristo Square. Then it went eastward along the Pleasance and the south side of College Street, till it crossed the Cowgate and followed the steep slope of St Mary's Wynd to the Netherbow on the ridge of the High Street. It then continued down the slope on the other side of the High Street till it reached the North Loch – still an excellent defence in its own right. The gate at the Netherbow was called the 'World's End' (where the World's End pub stands

The Canongate, just outside the Flodden Wall

today), and so it was, for nobody inside the wall wanted to venture outside.

All this effort was a pity, really, since the English didn't attack after all. What the wall did do was to completely enclose Edinburgh, and for an astonishing 250 years scarcely a house was erected outside the barricade. The walls were added to and strengthened whenever it looked like the English army might fancy another foray north, but the defences were never built much more than a mile long and a quarter of a mile wide. The area it encompassed was minute – and the whole of Edinburgh's population was stuck inside.

Suddenly every spare foot of space had to be utilised and houses reached heights of 130 feet. They were the first skyscrapers in the world and as tall as city architects dared erect them.

The grassy enclosures vanished under a rash of tenements, and the passages between these tenements narrowed until the closes were only a few feet wide – the term 'close' now meant exactly that. Everything was crammed together and there was no place left for the population to go, except down.

In the tenements a strange social structure developed. There was no question of one part of Edinburgh becoming a wealthy or fashionable district – rich and poor were all lumped in with each other. A tradesman could, if he chose, build his house right next to titled gentry – and the poor squeezed in wherever they could find a corner. In

Cleriheugh's Tavern, showing Old Town tenements

the end, however, the class system prevailed – as it usually does – and the buildings themselves became divided up according to social strata. A single tenement in Dixon's Close was inhabited by: a fishmonger on the ground floor; a lodging-house keeper on the first floor; the Dowager Countess of Balcarres on the second floor; and Mrs Buchan of Kello on the third floor. The floors above these contained milliners and mantua-makers (dressmakers) and the garrets or attics were filled with tailors and every other type of tradesman.

Of course, if you were really poor then you ended up in the cellars underneath.

In 1822, William Hazlitt called the Old Town a 'City of palaces, or of tombs – a quarry, rather than the habitation of men'. And Robert Louis Stevenson described it as 'for all the world like a rabbit warren, not only by the number of its dwellers but the complication of its passage and holes'.

It is hard to imagine the horrific conditions that existed in these underground chambers. In winter Edinburgh is wet, freezing and windy and within the bare stone walls of these dank and frosty cellars conditions must have been Arctic-like. Lighting fires warmed the inhabitants but filled the cellars with acrid smoke and represented a huge safety hazard as there were tons of timber directly above.

The threat of fire was a constant worry to city officials. The underground vaults, however, being made mainly of stone, were actually a safer place to light fires than in the timber houses above. In 1666, a Town Council edict proclaimed a fine of one hundred merks for anyone found baking bread in 'any high or loftit houses' instead of 'laich cellars or voltis upon the ground'. Underground inhabitants must have breathed a sigh of relief at this as burning tenements tended to collapse, thus burying the cellar occupants under a mountain of molten timber. But if winter was bad, summertime conditions were worse.

Edinburgh had no sewage system. The method of garbage disposal in the Old Town was to shout 'Gardy-loo' and throw everything out the window. Gardy-loo was a warped version of *gardez l'eau* (approximately French for 'watch out for the water') – except it wasn't just water the warning referred to. Effluence, sewage, dead cats, anything you didn't want in the house came out the window. It was a truly revolting method of waste disposal. If you lived in the town, of course, you knew about this and a cry of 'Gardy-loo' was greeted by the return screech of 'Haud yer haun' (hold your hand). This would give you time to get into a doorway and all you suffered was a few splatters. If you didn't live in Edinburgh and you heard a cry from above, you were quite likely to look up and see who was calling to you – which didn't do much for the tourist trade. In 1745 Edward Burt had a less than bird's-eye view of the horror of Edinburgh sewage.

A guide was assigned to me, who went before me to prevent my Disgrace, crying all the Way, with a loud Voice, Hud your Haunde. The opening up of a sash, or otherwise opening a Window, made me tremble, while behind me, at some little Distance, fell the terrible Shower.

The High Street itself, perched on top of a ridge, enjoyed relatively tolerable conditions – to some extent effluence drained off down the slope. Here the cellars or 'laigh booths' were somewhat more habitable and were even used by traders to sell their wares. Even so, residents had to cut channels through solid rubbish to get to their front doors. Since it wasn't in the High Street the liquid waste had to be draining off somewhere. In the narrow, festering closes behind the Royal Mile raw sewage was ankle-deep in the streets and the North Loch slowly turned into a stinking, fetid sewer. Living at ground level in the back tenements was a truly harrowing experience. But, if living at ground level was wretched, living in stinking, diseased and rat-infested underground chambers – with sewage seeping in from above – was unbearable. Yet people did bear it as there was no other place for them to go.

And still the tenements rose and the buildings crowded together until only thin strips of sky could be glimpsed between the towering lands and new levels were piled haphazardly on top of existing

Tailors' Hall, Cowgate

buildings. On a visit to Edinburgh, Dorothy Wordsworth, viewing the tenements, wrote that they 'hardly resembled the work of men, it is more like the piling up of rocks'.

Ground-floor inhabitants found their dwellings became the foundations for surrounding developments. Houses that had been open to the air were buried, cut off forever from the light of day, becoming part of the growing underground city. No matter how high the buildings were, no matter how much they encroached on each other, deeper living and storage spaces could be cut sideways into the rock. This warren effect, skyscrapers sprouting from different levels and virtual caves dotted in-between, must have been the ultimate in optical illusions. It prompted Robert Louis Stevenson's description of cellars 'high above the gazer's head'.

Buildings on the steep sides of the Mile were gloriously uneven at foundation level as well as haphazardly constructed at the higher levels. In 1775 Captain Edward Topham gave this account of the tenement structures.

> The style of the building here is much like the French: the houses, however, in general, are higher, as some rise to twelve, and one in particular to thirteen storeys in height. But to the front of the street nine or ten storeys is the common run; it is the back part of the edifice which, by being built on the slope of

a hill, sinks to that amazing depth, so as to
form the above number.

By the seventeenth century Edinburgh had
become an architectural nightmare and had earned
the reputation of being the worst city in Europe to
live. And still the people stayed. Outside the
Flodden Wall was just too dangerous a place to be.
There was no choice.

The Second Underground City – The Bridges

Scotland was a rough, barbaric country – medieval in character long after the Middle Ages had passed – and Edinburgh remained a walled city right up until the eighteenth century. The city was invaded as late as 1745 when it was captured by Bonnie Prince Charlie on his way south to try and regain the British throne. This bold conquest was always doomed and, a year later, Charles's Highland army was annihilated at Culloden. This was to be the last battle fought on the British mainland and peace came to Scotland at last. By the nineteenth century the formidable Flodden Wall was in ruins and the population could finally spread out on to the surrounding land. Then, however, Edinburgh suddenly faced a new problem.

Around the Old Town were seven hills, and the uneven camber of the land proved a severe hindrance to the city's expansion. But Edinburgh has always been a unique town and, true to form, the inhabitants came up with a unique solution to their problem. Though Castle Hill and Calton Hill still rise clear of their surroundings, the five neighbouring hills seemed to have vanished. This is not the case.

Moultree's Hill, Bunker's Hill, St John's Hill, St Leonard's Hill and Heriot Hill are still there – but hidden – their steepness brilliantly engineered out of existence. For, as Edinburgh expanded, the gaps between these hills were spanned by five giant bridges. And the ravines they spanned were to provide perfect conditions for a second underground city.

By the early nineteenth century, Edinburgh was undergoing something of a renaissance and had acquired the grandiose title 'Athens of the North'. The city led the world in medicine, law, philosophy, education and, most importantly, architecture. Edinburgh University started lectures in civil engineering in 1800 – almost a quarter of a century before the rest of Europe – and virtually all early civil engineers visited the city at some time. So, when it came to bridge-building, Edinburgh had no peers.

Five main bridges were built in the central area round the Old Town between 1765 and 1833.

North Bridge, South Bridge, George IV Bridge, Regent's Bridge and King's Bridge created an architectural vista that no other city could match. In 1905 the novelist G.K. Chesterton wrote in the *Daily News*:

> The beauty of Edinburgh as a city is absolutely individual, and consists in one separate atmosphere and one separate class of qualities. It consists chiefly in a quality that may be called 'abruptness', an unexpected alternation of heights and depths. It seems like a city built on precipices: a perilous city. Although the actual valleys and ridges are not (of course) really very high or very deep, they stand up like strong cliffs; they fall like open chasms. There are turns of the steep street that take the breath away like a literal abyss. There are thoroughfares, full, busy and lined with shops, which yet give the emotions of an alpine stair. It is, in the only adequate word for it, a sudden city.

This 'suddenness' is not due to the bridges alone, but to the astonishing way they were integrated into the city. These bridges were not simply built and left. They blended into existing streets. The gaps they spanned were filled in, developed and built up. Buildings were constructed above and on either side until the mighty structures were almost totally con-

George IV Bridge

cealed. And a mass of chambers and vaults that had been built underneath these bridges and into the hills they connected became completely invisible.

The vaults under the bridges were constructed for a simple reason – because they could be. Though it was a marvel of economical planning, building vaults into the supporting arches of each bridge was perfectly logical. Why fill in valuable storage space – especially in a city as crowded as Edinburgh – when engineers could now fill the underside of bridges with stone chambers? After all, empty chambers could be put to all sorts of uses.

And, as we will see, these hidden chambers were put to some uses the city planners could never have imagined.

Work began on the North Bridge in 1765 and a portion of the North Loch was drained to provide land for its construction. Despite Edinburgh's fine reputation for engineering, the first attempt collapsed and killed five workmen. But, by 1772, the rebuilt bridge was open. It measured 1,270 feet and was supported by three main arches, two smaller ones and a number of masked vaults. Even in 1774 some pretty strange uses had already been thought up for those vaults. For instance, magistrates of the time proclaimed that all beggars found

Cowgate Port (from a view by Ewbank, published in
1825)

in the streets should be imprisoned under the North Bridge and fed on bread and water.

Regent's Bridge (built to join Calton Hill to the east end of Princes Street and opened in 1818) and the King's Bridge (west of the Grassmarket and completed in 1833) are less central and have relatively few vaults below. More interesting are South Bridge and George IV Bridge – both connected to the Royal Mile.

George IV Bridge extends southward at right angles from the Lawnmarket, running across the Cowgate to a point near the south end of Candlemaker Row. Begun in 1827, it was finally completed in 1836 and is 300 yards in length. It has three, open-groined arches that can be seen from the Cowgate – but another eleven arches are completely hidden – closed up to make vaults for properties on either side of the bridge. Again, these vaults were put to many an odd use. On top of the bridge a sheriff court occupied the site where the National Library now stands, and officers used the buried chambers below to hold prisoners awaiting trial.

But of all the bridges one stands out in Edinburgh lore. Its vaults and chambers provide a wealth of stories that add hugely to the legend of the underground city: the South Bridge.

Niddry, Marlin and Peebles Wynds were swept away to create space for the building of the South Bridge and two higher streets (Blair Street and Hunter Square) were created beside it. The foundation stone was laid in 1785 and the bridge was opened to foot passage the next year. It had been built with astonishing speed. This giant structure is over 1,000 feet long and is, to all intents and purposes, invisible. One thirty-foot-high arch can be seen which spans the Cowgate at the foot of Niddry Street, but the other nineteen giant arches are completely hidden.

These arches were, as with the other bridges, divided into vaults and chambers and separated by tunnels. As with the other bridges, the vaults were supposed to be used as cellars and storehouses for local merchants and shopkeepers – and for much of the time they were. But there is an awful lot of space under the South Bridge and gradually the uses for the vaults diversified. Traders set up as cobblers, drapers, wine merchants and jewellers in the caverns. Some of the aristocracy used the chambers for drinking and debauchery and even for occult practices – part of a depraved fraternity known as the Hellfire Club.

However, conditions under the bridge were worsening. The top of the South Bridge might be lined with spacious and fashionable shops, but the area below had been abandoned by the Edinburgh gentry and was becoming an overcrowded slum. Worse still, traders began to realise that the builders of this magnificent edifice hadn't managed to make it waterproof – so they quickly moved out again and left the vaults to the slum dwellers.

Chambers Street

The vaults may have been cold and damp but, in winter, they were better than trying to survive on the streets. So people began living down there.

On the lowest point of the Old Town, between the South Bridge and George IV Bridge, the Cowgate valley lurked in the shadow of the High Street and the Bridges themselves. At one time this had been the most fashionable of suburbs: in the early-eighteenth century it housed two dukes, sixteen earls, seven lords, seventeen lords of session, thirteen baronets, three commanders-in-chief and a boarding school for young ladies. But they had long abandoned their old haunts and the poor had rushed into the vacuum. Before long the Grassmarket, on the other side of George IV Bridge, and in the shadow of the castle itself, had suffered the same fate. The tenements fell into disrepair and the warren of airless cellars that peppered the steep slopes of the High Street were filled to capacity.

One might ask why this was necessary. After all, by the end of the nineteenth century the Flodden Wall was a ruin and Edinburgh's New Town was spreading out to the north. Surely there was enough space for everyone in the city to live in some degree of comfort? To some extent there was – if you had money to pay for it.

The picturesque New Town – still breathtaking today – attracted the more affluent citizens and they deserted the Old Town in droves. This should have left more room for the poor who were left behind, but the opposite was true. A combination of economic and political factors meant that new immigrants were flooding into Edinburgh. Industrial and agricultural revolutions had caused mass unemployment in the countryside, but the city factories thrived on cheap labour and so attracted many people to the city. While famine compelled thousands of destitute Irish families to leave their native land and try to scrape a living in Scottish cities, in the north the Highland Clearances forced entire clans from their ancestral lands and those who did not emigrate had only one place to go: the city. Between 1800 and 1830, the population of Edinburgh doubled.

There was only one part of Edinburgh with enough cheap housing to accommodate such a flood of poverty-stricken immigrants: the slums of the Old Town. The crushed and crowded closes sloping away from the High Street became more overpopulated than they had ever been before. If anything, the conditions in the closes behind the Royal Mile were worse than in the Middle Ages. G.H. Martin's account of Edinburgh in the 1840s painted a bleak picture of the fate awaiting this tidal wave of unfortunate humanity.

> Wages were low because labour was readily
> attracted by the apparent wealth in the city,
> but accommodation was comparatively
> cheap because the old properties lent them-

selves, both in their structure and by social customs, to the repeated subdivision of tenements. It therefore became, for many of its immigrants, a social trap from which there was no escape but death.

Under the South Bridge, along the Cowgate and Grassmarket and in the tiny closes of the Royal Mile, the poor lived in conditions of astonishing deprivation. Many buildings were derelict and dangerous – their ownership forgotten – but people were crammed into them like sardines. Once again, there wasn't room in the Old Town to swing a rat. The underground city was thriving too and its cellars and vaults were teeming with beggars and urchins. Thanks to the warrens of vaults built into the bridges – and now filled with humankind – its domain was even larger than before. As late as 1850 there are accounts of families living under the ground in the Old Town in deplorable conditions. In 1845 George Bell MD – an early social reformer – published a horrific account of life in Blackfriar's Wynd, next to the South Bridge.

In a vault or cave under a large tenement, reside an old man, his invalid wife and his two daughters, one of whom has a natural child and the other of whom is paralytic. The man has an air of respectability about him, but the family has no visible means of living. There were three beds in the vault; and on investigating the matter, [we] found that the said vault is a lodging house, and is often tenanted to repletion. This man is the type of class who live by subletting their miserable and dark abodes to as many as can be crammed into them. In another vault in the wynd we found a very fat Irishwoman, a widow, a pauper and the mother of six children. By her own confession she occasionally takes in a lodger – in reality, however, she accommodates two or three all the year round.

The Castle Hill, 1845

Life in the
Underground City

The horrific conditions in the underground city, and the cramped and rotting tenements above, gave the valleys of the Cowgate and the Grassmarket, hidden in the shadow of the High Street, an incredible reputation for filth, poverty and crime. One can hardly imagine the despondency and discontent that afflicted the underground dwellers, entrenched in their dank dungeons with no hope of reprieve. The cellars of the Old Town were a social and physical prison from which there was no honest method of escape. One could spend years of backbreaking toil with virtually no reward, save the chance of moving into one of the better tenements – and, if those lands were in the same area, this was not much of an upturn in fortune. In a climate where unemployment was rife and no job secure there was always the distinct possibility that, no matter how hard you worked, you could end up back in the underground city again. There were no unions to look after the fortunes of the workers in those days. You could toil in a factory from six in the morning to ten at night and if you complained, someone else would willingly take your job.

The treatment of the industrial workers was astonishing. In nail factories boys could have their earlobes nailed to a board if too many of the spikes they produced were bent. In the Lothian mines young women helped to haul coal carts through the suffocating darkness using harnesses that eventually warped and twisted their bodies to the point where many became hunchbacks. Boys were employed to sit far underground, guarding the fire flaps that punctuated the long dark tunnels. These boys would crouch in the dark in cramped and freezing conditions for hours at a time waiting for the rumble of a coal cart. Then they would pull a rope to lift the flap and allow the cart through, before lowering the barrier again. After that it was back to the lonely vigil, trying desperately to keep fear, claustrophobia and, most of all, sleep at bay. For if the long monotonous hours and the early rising got too much for a young lad, he might fall asleep where he sat and tumble forward on to the tracks. And if his exhaustion was too deep to rouse him to let him hear the rumble of the next approaching coal cart he would be cut in two.

Reformers, of course, tried to improve the conditions of those whose working lives almost matched the horrors of where they lived. For many years, however, even after reforms passed into law, the conditions in the mines remained little changed. As with so many other areas of industry, the money to be made was too great and the lives of the people making that money for their employers were too cheap.

In desperation some reformers even sent a sketch artist down the mines, to see if pictures could indeed take the place of a thousand condemning words. The sketches showed the criminal conditions where men, women, girls and boys laboured in misery, and the desperation is clearly etched on their faces. Yet the mine owners were unmoved and the lethargy of the public did not bode well for the workers.

That is, until someone pointed out one picture. It showed a teenage boy and girl being pulled out of the mine on a rough pulley system. The pulley was no more than a stout rope with a bar fastened on one end. In order to stay on this precarious perch, the teenagers had to sit opposite each other, pressed together. And, since they had both been labouring hard in the confines of the narrow mines, neither had a great deal of clothing on.

One must remember that these were Victorian times. The idea of half-clothed teenagers sitting so close together was unthinkable. It just wasn't done.

The public outcry was so great that many of the mine practices were changed immediately.

If the conditions in the mines were bad, the lot of the chimney sweeps was even worse. The huge tenements of the Royal Mile were made of wood and the chimneys had to be swept continually to ensure that the coal dust did not build up and lead to a conflagration. In the eighteenth and nineteenth centuries the Old Town was an ocean of chimneys arrayed at dizzying heights under an eternal pall of smoke. It was a view of which Victorian nightmares were made and provided a constant source of revenue, as well as a continual challenge, for the city sweeps.

There was differing apparatus that could be used to clean the city 'lums' – including systems of elongated hinged poles and a pulley apparatus invented in Edinburgh. But many of the chimneys were not straight up and down but were twisted and angled, mirroring the haphazard construction of the tenements themselves. The bends also prevented falls of soot right into the room below. To clean a narrow, soot-blocked, twisting chimney with any kind of mechanism, no matter how ingenious, was a costly and time-consuming task. Children were a far faster and cheaper apparatus for carrying out this task – and the smaller they were the better.

To begin with, life as a chimney sweep in Edinburgh wasn't all that bad. Sweeps tended to use their own children in a sort of apprenticeship and so tried to avoid letting them be killed. But, as always, greed overcame human compassion. In the Old Town orphanages there was an enormous supply of kids and even more in the underground city. Many families, living in abject poverty, simply couldn't afford their own offspring and abandoned them or sold them into hard labour. There was a reservoir of unclaimed youth that the sweeps could dip into any time they pleased.

By the late 1700s a chimney sweep in old Edinburgh could be employed as young as four years old and, if he was, his life expectancy was six months. The limb joints of the children were rubbed with special preparations, each sweep had his own, then heated in front of a roaring fire to harden the skin – but it did little good. If a sweep lived past his twelfth birthday his body would already be deformed by the constant pushing of his young limbs against the brick walls. Many childhood sweeps needed crutches to walk by the time they reached adulthood and, of course, were then unfit for any other kind of job. The forced tolerance to heat, however, often came in handy since many households didn't put the fires out while the child was up the chimney. Rather, it would be allowed to smoulder, to make it easier to light properly once the chimney was swept.

The treatment of young sweeps was quite often astonishing. There is a record of two master sweeps working Edinburgh's New Town in the early-nineteenth century whose method of getting children up and down chimneys was to tie a rope to their arms and legs and then just pull in the direction they wanted the unfortunate child to go. This allowed their children to get to the roof and back without getting the furniture and carpets of the nice New Town houses dirty. It also gave the master sweeps the added bonus that the child's body partially swept the chimney as he was dragged through it. The men were eventually prosecuted for their cruelty, which was excessive even in those times.

The great fear of every chimney sweep was to get stuck in a chimney. There were various reasons why this might happen, each one as horrible as the other. The chimney might narrow causing the child to get his shoulders stuck and so lose the climbing and manoeuvring power of his arms. Rain might leak into the top making the shaft impossible to climb. The sweep might get jammed trying to twist his body round one of the many chimney bends. Worst of all, he might be hit by a fall of soot. This not only restricted the boy's movements and added a huge weight to the climb, it often cut off the child's sight and even his breathing.

There were several methods employed to free a trapped sweep. The most humane was to knock away the brickwork of the chimney breast nearest to where the panicked child was screaming and try and get him out through the hole. However, this took some time and was frowned upon in more expensive houses. An easier method was simply to send another child up to rescue him. The second child might take a birch to slap the feet of his companion above or even a small lighted branch as added incentive. This method of rescue involved the possibility of the second child getting stuck too, and even a third. In theory, it would be quite possible to have an entire chimney full of trapped sweeps – though there is no record of this ever happening. But, just in case, the ever-enterprising master sweep always had Plan B to hand. Building up the fire in the grate below the child sometimes spurred him into frenzied action and, if that failed, they could always attach a rope to the child's leg and haul him back down. This type of rescue might result in the death of that particular child or the snapping of his limbs or vertebrae – but there were plenty more where he came from.

Living in the dark, sewage-splattered vaults meant earning a few pennies while being worked half to death or slowly starving while begging in the streets. Life in the underground city and the surrounding slums was the ultimate in poverty traps. Honesty didn't seem to pay and so the underground city had more than its fair share of villains. In the immensely claustrophobic condi-

The Guard House and Black Turnpike

tions, everybody knew everyone else, yet the population was so huge it was impossible to keep track of who lived where, what they did and where they did it. The criminal fraternity were in their element underground: thousands of dark cellars, bridge vaults joined by myriad tunnels, tiny, twisting closes in every direction and thousands of bodies in the darkness, dressed in identical rags. If you wanted to hide from the law or conduct any kind of illegal enterprise, the underground city was the place to do it. As Alexander Smith put it: 'The people of the Cowgate seldom visit the upper streets,' and the reverse was also true. The vaults of the South Bridge, the cellars of the Grassmarket and the rickety tenements above, the vaults and laigh booths of the Royal Mile and the tiny closes

sloping down into the fetid trench of the Cowgate –
all this became the domain of thieves, prostitutes,
debauched aristocrats, bodysnatchers and murderers.

Up until the nineteenth century there was no real
police force to staunch this tide of sin. Edinburgh
was patrolled by the 'Town Guard', which consisted
mainly of retired soldiers from Highland regiments
who were not known for sympathetic policing.
Their main function, anyway, was not so much
detective work and crime solving as crowd-control
– the Edinburgh 'mob' was famed and feared. With
so many dissatisfied people crammed into one
squalid space it was possible for a riot to materialise
at the drop of a hat. Hangings, especially, caused a
huge furore, with the crowd screaming for the
prisoner to be hanged faster or released altogether,
depending how sympathetic they felt that day. The
Town Guard had the unenviable task of keeping the
mob under control, which they seemed to do by
applying brute force at every opportunity. They
were constantly the target of jeers and missiles, no
matter what the social occasion, and, not
surprisingly, things sometimes got a little out of
hand

On one occasion in 1736 a smuggler named
Wilson was hanged in the Grassmarket after
tackling three guards and holding on to them so his
accomplice could escape. The crowd quickly heard
of Wilson's bravado and decided it was unfair to
hang so spirited a fellow. The hanging quickly

The Tolbooth, Edinburgh's prison

turned into a riot and the mob began flinging stones at the Town Guard. The captain of the Guard, John Porteous, ordered his men to open fire. In the set-to five or six of the mob were killed and about twenty were injured. For this over-enthusiastic peacekeeping Porteous was arrested, condemned to death and held in the Tolbooth prison in Parliament Square – but was then reprieved by Queen Caroline. On hearing the good news the mob quickly formed again, stormed the Tolbooth, dragged Porteous back to the Grass-market and hanged him. Then they simply melted back into the closes and cellars. Not one person was arrested for the Porteous murder.

Even after a rudimentary police force was estab-lished in Edinburgh, the underground city con-tinued to be a stronghold for villains. A bastion where, though not immune from the law, wrong-doers of every hue could hide and plot and strike. Robert Louis Stevenson paints an inimitable portrait of life in that area in his description of 'loiterers'.

> You go under dark arches and down dark
> stairs and alleys. The way is so narrow that
> you can lay a hand on either wall: so steep
> that, in greasy weather, the pavement is

almost as treacherous as ice . . . and the pavements are encumbered with loiterers.

These loiterers are a true character on the scene. Some shrewd Scotch workmen may have paused on their way to a job, debating Church affairs and politics with their tools upon their arm. But the most part are a different order – skulking jail birds; unkempt, bare-foot children; big-mouthed, robust women, in a sort of uniform of striped flannel petticoat and short tartan shawl: among these, a few supervising con-stables and a dismal sprinkling of mutineers and broken men from higher ranks in society, with some mark of better days upon them, like a brand.

Where Is It Now?

It was social reform, several particularly destructive fires and a housing disaster that finally put an end to the underground city. The first death knell for the warren of slums came in 1824 with the Great Fire of Edinburgh. It wasn't the first giant fire to ravage the Old Town – there were massive blazes in 1544, 1676, 1700 and 1725 – but the blaze of 1824 was on an unprecedented scale. It began in Old Assembly Close and spread to engulf the whole of the upper Royal Mile, from Parliament Square to Hunter Close. It raged with such fury that it took three days to extinguish, and caused devastation to the packed wooden tenements lining the main thoroughfare. Even the mighty Tron Kirk succumbed, its great wooden spire eventually collapsing on to the street.

Unfortunate though the fire was, in many

Fleshmarket Close, 1845

respects it marked the beginning of significant improvements in the Old Town. The first municipal fire brigade in Britain was founded by James Braidwood that same year as a direct result of the conflagration (he then went on to start the London Fire Brigade). But, equally importantly, many of the tallest and most dangerous tenements had been cleared away. Chinks of light were finally beginning to wind their way into the denseness of the humanity on the Royal Mile. Though the Grassmarket and Cowgate had not been touched, their demise, too, was a little closer.

The second disaster on the High Street occurred at Trotter's House, a high, stone tenement in Bailie Fyfe's Close. The house had stood for 250 years, but on 24 November 1861 it suddenly collapsed in the middle of the night burying thirty-five people. Locals rushed from their houses at the sound of the horrific crash and began to dig frantically at the rubble in a vain search for survivors. From under a pile of beams they heard the voice of a young boy. As they dug towards him he shouted: 'Heave awa' lads, I'm no deid yet!' They eventually pulled him out of the debris alive. The story is a famous one in Edinburgh and the close is often called Heave Awa' Land. The boy's valiant words and a sculpture of his face are still above the entrance. But the collapse of Trotter's House, like the Great Fire, heralded inevitable changes. Slowly but surely, housing improvements began. The worst tenements were pulled down and the citizens encouraged to move.

As the nineteenth century neared its end, so did the underground city. The cramped and crowded lands were pulled down and the old cellars abandoned, filled in or built over. The vaults under the bridges were evacuated and many were sealed off.

It's true that what is out of sight can very easily be put out of mind and the underground city soon passed into legend.

Today the story has grown and, as with all urban myths, tenuously related factors have added to its stature. Anything found anywhere in the city that was built before living memory and just happens to be under the surface becomes grist for the mill in the underground city legend. Here is a perfect example. In Gilmerton there was a man-made cave, dug out of stone by a George Paterson, a forty-foot passage with rooms on either side and tables and benches carved from the rock. It was described by the Rev Thomas Whyte, the parish minister of Liberton, in 1792 as carved:

> . . . out of the rock in the nicest manner.
> Here there was a forge with a well and a
> washing house. Here there were several
> windows which communicated light from
> above. The author of this extraordinary piece
> of workmanship after he had finished it,
> lived in it for a long time with his wife and
> family and prosecuted his business as a
> smith. He died in it about the year 1735.

A nice story, but nothing at all to do with any underground city. Besides, Gilmerton isn't even near the Old Town. Not only that but the cave was investigated in 1897 by F.R. Coles, assistant keeper of the National Museum of Antiquities in Scotland, who cast grave doubt over whether Paterson had been responsible. He found: 'The method of cutting stone pointed to an origin much more remote than the eighteenth century and the substantial work involved in excavating the cave could not have been carried out by one man.' But mystery only adds to the lore of a place and, as Rev Whyte added: 'His cave for many years was deemed as a great curiosity and visited by all the people of fashion.'

Though it has no link to the real underground city at all, that kind of fame makes for one more, albeit tiny, piece of the puzzle.

As we have seen, much of the underground city bore no resemblance to any other kind of city and much of it wasn't even strictly underground. Such was the structure of the Old Town dwellings and their substructure that, pushing between the dark, crowded tenements, the line between what was 'below' and 'above' ground was completely erased.

People do whisper of underground tunnels running under all of Edinburgh, not just the Old Town, and this is true to some extent. Apart from the legendary castle tunnels there are, for example, sewage tunnels under Princes Street – but this occurs in most cities. Stranger perhaps are the tunnels running under Calton Hill and the New Town. These are a result of 'railway mania' in the nineteenth century.

As the railway replaced the canal as the transportation of the future in Edinburgh's imagination, new train lines sprang up all over the city. In 1836 plans were approved for the Edinburgh, Leith and

Newhaven Railway. The line travelled through a tunnel running from the east end of Princes Street all the way under the New Town to Scotland Street. In 1842 the North British Railway Company constructed another massive tunnel underneath Calton Hill and dug ventilation shafts all the way along it. These shafts are occasionally stumbled upon when excavation or development work is being done in the area, and are often mistaken for underground streets. There are buried dwellings in the Calton Hill area, especially around Regent's Bridge, but the rail tunnels were never occupied – and not that many trains ran through them.

The Old Town is the real site of the underground city. It is the site of Mary King's Close and Marlin's Wynd, the bridges and their vaults, the High Street, Cowgate and Grassmarket cellars and the castle vaults and tunnels (if there are any).

It is a conglomeration of these things that make up the map of an underground city. But the skeleton of fact is fleshed out by generations of weird and wonderful stories, and tiny fragments of what might be down there join together to complete a mythical picture. The fragment may be small but impressive – like the remains of Marlin's Wynd, embedded in the floor of the Tron Kirk. It may be completely out of sight, like Mary King's Close. Its very existence may be doubtful – like the castle tunnel under the High Street. It may be all those things, like St Margaret's Well.

The Grassmarket and Castle Rock

St Margaret's Well was guarded by the Well House Tower, a ruin standing at the foot of Castle Rock on the edge of the North Loch. The tower was built as part of the defences when the wall of 1450 was erected round the Old Town. Today it is the only remaining part of the defence that can still be seen. Many years ago, so popular legend relates, a set of steps was discovered underneath piles of debris at the foot of the tower. The steps were hewn out of solid stone and led to a secret passage with a thick, fortified door at the end. It was theorised that this was intended as a sallyport (a gateway which allowed people to move from a fortified place) in connection with an underground passage winding down from the castle. The castle garrison could then safely send men down to collect water without fear of being attacked. Of course, today, there is no sign of the stone steps. But if they did exist, they might well be buried again to hide the secret way into the castle. So the speculation continues and the legend of castle tunnels and, ultimately, the underground city suffers not a bit from it.

On the High Street you can still track down the sites of the stories contained in these pages. In some cases, as has been said, there is nothing to see – and some popular conceptions of what is 'down there' are rather misguided. It is popularly thought, for instance, that the famous preacher, John Knox, is still buried in a graveyard under the car park in Parliament Square (under parking space number forty-four, in fact). There is a little yellow square marking the spot. In reality, the graveyard was moved years ago, and poor John Knox's remains could be just about anywhere. But, as so often happens, there is a grain of truth behind the legend.

Parliament House (at the back of Parliament Square) was begun in 1632. The building did not lend itself to economical construction, for the steep slope plummeting to the Cowgate behind entailed a considerable amount of under building – only a portion of which could be used. As with so many buildings on the High Street, ground level at the front could be storeys high at the back – making the bottom back level, in effect, underground. Burton's *Life of Hume* vividly records this Alice-in-Wonderland effect.

> Entering one of the doors opposite the main entrance, the stranger is led . . . down flight after flight of the steps of a stone staircase, and when he imagines he is descending far into the bowels of the earth, he emerges on the edge of a cheerful, crowded thorough-fare, connecting together the old and new town . . . When he looks up to the building containing the upright street through which he has descended, he sees that vast pile of tall houses standing at the head of the Mound which creates astonishment in every visitor of Edinburgh.

In the same manner, the main building of Parliament House has three 'storeys': the Great Hall, the subterranean Laich House and a vaulted, stone undercroft – inaccessible and even further underground. A similar example, Mary King's Close, is on the other side of the High Street. It too is underground – covered over by the City Chambers in the mid-eighteenth century – yet the other end could still be entered at street level until the early-twentieth century. Even today, the steep gradient of

Victoria Street and Terrace from George IV Bridge

the Royal Mile means that the south side of the close is completely underground but the north side is level with Cockburn Street, but at that end it is simply blocked off.

Though the foundations of Parliament Square cannot be reached, Mary King's Close is open to the public. So is Marlin's Wynd – once buried underneath the Tron Kirk but now excavated. There may well be other things down there waiting to be discovered. In 1844 workmen clearing the steeply sloping ground at the rear of Parliament Square found a buried piece of the Flodden Wall and several ancient stone coffins.

Unfortunately, the majority of the old underground city is gone for good. Edinburgh Castle is still a military garrison and, as such, unlikely to admit to any tunnels running from it under the High Street – just in case some terrorist uses one to blow the castle up. The Flodden Wall, cause of so much of the underground city, is also mostly gone. There are places, however, where sections still stand. There is a section inside Greyfriars churchyard, one in the Vennel above the Grassmarket and a section opposite the Pleasance. If you walk down the High Street to the World's End pub and look at the cobbled road outside, you can see brass slabs marking the gateway that separated the Old Town from the far more vulnerable Canongate.

The original tenements of the High Street, Cowgate and Grassmarket are mostly destroyed,

Lord Cockburn Street and the back of the Royal Exchange

and any cellars that haven't been filled in are used as plain old cellars again – they belong to the houses and shops above. There is scant surface evidence of the past horrors of living below ground. Yet it is only in the Old Town that a shop assistant can descend into a cellar, move a few boxes and find a fireplace or the outline of a door or window leading absolutely nowhere.

Today, the most easily seen parts of the underground city are the vaults underneath the South Bridge. Pubs like Whistle Binkies, The Bare Story and Bannermans are built into the Bridge's foundations, and some of the larger vaults have been converted into nightclubs – not a use the original builders could possibly have foreseen!

But, behind these establishments, more tunnels and chambers exist in their original form. These dark, foreboding vaults were opened to the public for the first time in 1994 – and have added considerably to the underground legend. Ghostly goings-on, it would appear, are rife in this newly reopened section. And this is one thing that all parts of Edinburgh's underground city seem to have in common: they are all reputed to be haunted.

There are endless ghost stories set in old Edinburgh – it seems sometimes every spirit in Scotland has taken up residence there – and many of these spooky tales take place underground. The rest of the book relates the stories, whether supernatural or corporeal, factual or mythical, that brought about and added to the legend of Edinburgh's underground city. In most cases, the original locations can be found on the Royal Mile.

Happy hunting.

PART TWO

*Tales from the
Underground City*

Marlin's Wynd

One of the oldest and most interesting sections of the underground city is the recently excavated Marlin's Wynd which is underneath the floor of the Tron Kirk on the Royal Mile. The central walking space inside the church has been removed and, during the summer months, visitors can see the ancient thoroughfare underneath.

Marlin's Wynd was typical of many Old Town streets. It was crowded, bustling and diverse – housing corn and poultry markets and littered with book stores and stalls. Built in 1532, it is generally acknowledged to be the first paved walkway in the city. And, as with all the streets of Old Edinburgh, Marlin's Wynd has its own peculiar legend. John Marlin, a Frenchman, was so proud of being the paver of Edinburgh's first cobbled street that he asked to be buried underneath it. He believed the

New Year's Eve at the Tron Kirk

wynd would stand forever and remain a fine monument to his memory. According to his wishes he was buried at the head of the street that still bears his name and his tomb was marked for posterity by six flat stones in the shape of a grave.

But John Marlin didn't foresee the incessant construction that was to transform the Royal Mile. Where his bones rest now is anybody's guess. One half of his street was buried when the Tron Kirk was built over it in 1637 and the other half was demolished in 1786 to make way for the South Bridge. Worse still for the memory of the unfortunate Frenchman, is a perfectly legitimate claim that another Old Town street was paved three years before by two of Marlin's fellow countrymen – John and Bartoulme Foliot. This pair lie buried in Holyrood Chapel – a far more conventional resting place.

Still, fate has a strange way of catapulting its forgotten heroes back into the historical limelight. John Marlin became famous again after the floor of the Tron Kirk was removed in the 1970s, and – almost half a millennium after his death – his long-buried wynd is now visible. The Foliots, on the other hand, have become mere footnotes in Edinburgh's history – their cobbled creation yet another of the city's buried and forgotten thoroughfares.

Mary King's Close

Of all the streets and closes in the city, buried or otherwise, Mary King's Close stands out in Edinburgh lore. Though it is now hidden below Edinburgh Council's City Chambers, the street still exists and is now open to visitors. Little is known about Mary King herself, and the close might have slipped into history just as unremarkably had it not been for the plague of 1645.

The cramped and filthy conditions inside the Flodden Wall provided a perfect breeding ground for disease, and when the plague inevitably arrived Edinburgh was devastated. Before the pestilence struck, the population in the city was around 40,000; by the time the plague had finished, only sixty citizens were registered fit to carry arms and defend the city. Naturally, an epidemic of this magnitude caused panic among city officials and often their dubious solution was to wall up any area where the dreaded sickness broke out. On one occasion, the Council sealed up a plague-stricken nursery – with the children still trapped inside the building. The mothers, discovering what had happened, left their workplaces and raced down the High Street – begging for food, water and blankets – anything that could provide some comfort for their doomed offspring. When the women reached the nursery, the Council allowed them inside to be with their terrified children. Then they walled the mothers up too.

Legend has it that a similar fate befell Mary King's Close, which was closed up while the inhabitants lay dying inside. When – two months later – the City Council felt it was safe to remove the bodies, rigor mortis had taken hold. Wearing herb-filled masks (a useless safeguard as the plague was transmitted by rat mites), Council workers dismembered the corpses with axes and hauled the remains away in carts. The victims were buried outside the city walls in the area now known as The Meadows – these days a particularly green and fertile park. The Council's deeds earned the ill-fated street the nickname 'Bloody Mary's Close' – and the legends about it grew wilder and wilder.

Though the plague soon passed, Mary King's Close remained closed and, as years went by, the street became a place of mystery and dread. Open one of these long closed doors, it was whispered, and the deadly fingers of disease would once more grip the city. This, of course, was not true, but mystery breeds fear – and fear spreads as fast as any plague. According to folklore of the time, Mary King's Close quickly became a hotbed of ghostly activity. If you looked through the derelict windows late at night, you could spy on long-dead inhabitants going about their normal business – apparently blissfully unaware that they were deceased. It was also reported that the majority of these phantom residents were missing heads or other assorted limbs – thus discouraging would-be peeping Toms even more. According to Edinburgh folklore, two ministers were among the few living beings brave enough to enter the street – boasting that the power of their faith could overcome any supernatural obstacles. The first obstacles they encountered, however, turned out to be a ravaged bloody face and severed arm thrusting through the wall of the close. Worse still, the arm was flourishing a sword above the ministers' heads. The unshakeable faith of these men of God was obviously somewhat shaken by the encounter – they turned on their heels and ran.

In 1685, *Satan's Invisible World* was published by George Sinclair, Professor of Moral Philosophy at Glasgow University. This was a chronicle of medieval devilment – a bit of a bestseller in those days – and it contained several stories concerning Mary King's Close. If the population of Edinburgh had been wary of Bloody Mary's Close before, these florid chronicles ensured the street a real place in Scottish infamy as a Wynd from Hell – not to mention being the ultimate in housing problems.

Many years after the plague had gone, an attempt was made by Edinburgh Council to re-inhabit certain sections of Mary King's Close. Given the city's chronic overcrowding this should have been an extremely easy task. According to Professor Sinclair, a lawyer named Thomas Coltheart was one of the first to move into the street. His maid, knowing the reputation of the place, promptly resigned, but Thomas Coltheart and his wife were made of sterner stuff.

One Sunday, as Mrs Coltheart sat reading the scriptures, a disembodied head – complete with long grey beard – floated across the room. Thomas Coltheart must have been either asleep or looking in the other direction because he missed it and, quite naturally, he found his wife's account a little hard to accept. But that night, as the couple climbed into bed, the phantom appeared again – and this time Thomas Coltheart saw it too. The startled tenants immediately began praying to God, the Heavens and anyone else who might be listening, but this only infuriated the spirits more. The head was joined by other apparitions: children, animals, severed limbs and many other monstrous forms. One hand, naked from the elbow, seemed intent on shaking hands with Mrs Coltheart. Mrs Coltheart declined.

Then, as suddenly as they came, the ghosts were gone.

Tom Coltheart was either incredibly brave, completely stupid or terminally lazy – for he refused to move house and remained in Mary King's Close until he died. Mrs Coltheart's views on the matter are not recorded.

But the Coltheart's stubbornness had obviously angered the spirit world, and the ghosts of the close took their revenge. At the moment Thomas Coltheart passed away, a family friend, living ten miles away in Tranent, woke to see 'something like a cloud' floating through his room. The cloud materialised into the miserable disembodied head of the unfortunate Tom Coltheart. It would seem he had finally been accepted by the other inhabitants of Bloody Mary's Close.

Edinburgh Council – finding it difficult to persuade prospective homeowners that Mary King's Close was prime real estate – began offering houses rent-free in an attempt to encourage people to move there. When one old soldier moved in with his wife, the couple found themselves sharing living quarters with a number of diced body parts. This pair had the good sense to move immediately, and Mary King's Close was abandoned for ever.

In 1750, a fire destroyed the south storeys of the close and a few years later the Royal Exchange was

The Heart of Midlothian, opposite Mary King's Close

built over the top. The Council were hoping that traders would use the new covered site as a market. But merchants were reluctant to set up stalls over the most haunted place in Edinburgh and stayed in front of St Giles Kirk on the other side of the Royal Mile.

Though the south side of the close was now underground, the north side (backing on to what is now Cockburn Street) was still accessible. However, by 1845 the whole street was in ruins and eventually it was blocked off completely.

And that's the famous legend of Mary King's Close, passed down for hundreds of years. Unfortunately, none of it is true.

In 2003, Mary King's Close was taken over by a company called the Continuum Group, who opened it to the public as The Real Mary King's Close. They began exhaustive research into the history of the close and came up with a rather different story from the celebrated one.

According to their research, there is no evidence of a devastating fire in 1750. Most astonishingly, there is no evidence that plague victims were locked inside and left to die. Instead, Edinburgh Council appointed doctors to the sufferers, gave them bread and ale and quarantined them at Sciennes or Boroughmuir.

As for the close being deserted in the eighteenth century then completely closed over? The last inhabitant was a saw-maker named Andrew Chesney who finally left in 1901.

But the haunted stories continue.

For instance, strange scratching noises can be heard behind the walls of the subterranean houses. Some believe the sounds are made by the ghost of a chimney sweep who died, trapped in one of the close's chimneys. Others think it is the spirit of a child sealed up with his family during the plague who, in a desperate attempt to escape his diseased prison, attempted to climb a chimney to freedom and got stuck.

In the depths of the close, one room has its very own spectre. 'Annie' is the ghost of a little girl and she haunts the kitchen of the old Royal Exchange coffee house. Her presence was discovered by a psychic who 'saw' a lonely figure standing in a corner of the room. The child looked so sad and lost that the psychic returned with a doll to cheer her up. It seemed to work. Annie has now been seen by several people – she seems to like the company – and it has become a custom for visitors to leave a little doll as a gift for the friendly ghost.

There is now quite a collection of figurines gathering dust down there and it makes either a touching sight or an extremely creepy one, depending on your frame of mind.

The original dismembered inhabitants of Mary King's Close rarely seem to haunt the area these days – but they do have the occasional ghostly knees-up (severed ones presumably). A group of nurses spent the night in the close as part of a charity drive and, next day, they were asked if any of the party had been kept awake by spooky goings-on. No, they replied grumpily, the only thing that had disturbed their sleep was the merrymaking from the pub above. They were horrified to learn that the only building over them was the City Chambers, which was shut for the night and quiet as the grave. The first residents of Mary King's Close don't appear to have abandoned their old home after all. They simply keep themselves to themselves.

The Site Where Scotland Died

On 25 March 1707 the Treaty of Union was ratified – a pact with England that effectively ended Scotland's right to govern itself. It was an act abhorred by Scotland's population – the decision of a few corrupt politicians motivated by greed. So unpopular was this move, considered by most Scots to be the death of their nation, that the Treaty of Union had to be signed in secret.

But where exactly was it signed? Furious mobs roamed Edinburgh's streets trying to find the place where the Duke of Queensbury, the Chancellor and rapacious parliament members might be ratifying the document. The crowd was desperate to break in and stop the signing going ahead and emotions were at fever pitch. If Queensbury's secret signing place could be located, the general population were more than ready to tear the so-called traitors limb from limb. Underground seemed like a perfect place to hide.

Three sites were considered the most likely spots where the Treaty of Union was finally ratified – and two of them were below the streets. The third was a small arbour (still standing) in the garden of Moray House in the Canongate. Moray House was just beyond the Flodden Wall and furthest away from the angry masses, but the arbour does seem a very exposed site for so secret an assignation.

Incidentally, there are cellars under Moray House (now a teacher-training college) and they are a perfect example of how quickly the hidden chambers are forgotten. Recently, Edinburgh Council launched an energy-conservation study to cut costs in the building and unearthed an electricity meter hidden behind a locked cellar door. It had not been read for fourteen years and landed the college with a potential bill of thousands of pounds.

Some accounts state that the signing took place in the cellar of Alexander Borthwick's tavern which stood in the south-west corner of Milne's Square (now Milne's Court). Certainly, the warren of underground cellars in that area would have made

Milne's Square, now Milne's Court

an excellent hiding place, and Edinburgh Castle was within sprinting distance should the conspirators be discovered. Sadly for historical sleuths, many of the original cellars were destroyed and replaced by the vaults of North Bridge Street in 1787.

In fact, very little is left under Milne's Court – though there were once five underground levels there. In the early years of this century Edinburgh

University decided to fill in the bottom levels to reinforce the foundations of the buildings above. Workmen filled in the wrong level, causing it to collapse into vaults even further underground. This made the foundations of Milne's Court more unstable than they had ever been, and the rest of the levels had to be filled in to compensate this.

The third, and most likely, location for the signing of the treaty is the cellar of 177 High Street – the Union Cellar. Though the house above is long gone, the exact location – right across the street from the Tron Church – is very easy to pinpoint. It is now the site of a restaurant.

There is a rather grisly footnote to the signing of the Treaty of Union. The Duke of Queensbury had a son, James Earl of Drumlanrig, noted in old peerages to have 'died young'. In fact, this was another cover-up by the Duke – his son was mentally subnormal and confined to a ground-floor room in Queensbury House (now Queensbury Hospital in the Canongate). This son was a rabid and gluttonous giant, and the windows of his room were permanently boarded up to stop anyone catching a glimpse of his hulking form. On the day the Duke left to sign the Treaty of Union he took most of his household with him – probably for protection. Hearing that things were unusually quiet in the great house, the monstrous Earl of Drumlanrig broke out of his confinement and roamed the empty corridors – until the enticing smell of cooking drew him to the kitchen. There he found a child turning that evening's roast on a spit over the fire.

When the Duke of Queensbury returned home from his treacherous mission he found his son roasting the half-eaten kitchen boy on the spit instead.

The Drummer Boy

One of Edinburgh's most famous underground legends revolves around the discovery of a tunnel in the dungeons of Edinburgh Castle in the early-nineteenth century. The City Council was curious to find out where this newly unearthed passage went, but the entrance wasn't large enough to allow exploration – unless the explorer happened to be a particularly small one.

Since there were no midgets in the vicinity, the Council decided to send a ten-year-old boy into the tiny aperture to see where the tunnel went to. This may sound like a heartless thing to do, but in those days, thousands of orphans were employed to climb inside chimneys and sweep them – so many Edinburgh children were used to crawling through small, dark spaces. To be fair to the councilmen, they did give the lad a tiny drum – and told him to beat it as he went. That way they could monitor his progress.

The child wriggled into the cold, black passage and wormed his way out of sight, frantically beating the drum. As the faint rat-tat-tat sound travelled under the High Street, councilmen followed safely along on top, listening to the poor lad's progress. At a spot just short of the Tron Church the drumming stopped. It did not start up again.

Edinburgh Council had a dilemma. Though life was cheap among the city's slum children they couldn't keep sending ten-year-old after ten-year-old into the tunnel – there was no telling how many they might get through. Instead, the Council quietly sealed the entrance back up. It was never reopened.

Does the tunnel still exist? Did it ever exist? Or is it simply a fairy-tale to scare unruly ten-year-olds? Edinburgh Castle is a military garrison and is hardly likely to give away details or even acknowledge the existence of a passage running right under its fortifications. But it does seem entirely possible that such a tunnel is real. The Castle was often under siege, and many ancient fortifications used secret passages to sneak messages and important persons through enemy blockades. The structure of the Old Town makes Edinburgh Castle a prime candidate for just such a tunnel.

It is certainly true that many excavations went on in the Castle's foundations. There are many deep, dark and horrible dungeons down there – hewn partly from solid rock – some are still on display to Castle visitors. It is also known that a secret passage, now lost to antiquity, existed on the north bank of Castle Hill and was guarded by the Well House Tower – fragments of which still exist. The legend itself takes many forms. In one popular version it is a bagpiper who was sent underground. This version seems rather dubious – if a burly soldier with a set of pipes could fit into a tunnel there wouldn't be many people who couldn't. Robert Louis Stevenson agrees with this analysis, calling this version 'a silly story'. In all the adaptations of the tale, however, the existence of the Castle tunnel is the constant factor – the drummer boy simply seems the most plausible rendering.

And local residents will tell you that on some nights, if there is no traffic around, a faint but frantic drumming can be heard below the streets around the Tron Kirk. In 1994, a woman on a private tour of underground vaults collapsed after hearing the drummer-boy story. When she came to, she told her astonished companions the reason for her fainting fit. She had heard a drumming behind her just before the story was told.

The Worst Poet in the World

By the nineteenth century the once affluent Cowgate had become a dark, claustrophobic chasm of shadows. Crammed between the South Bridge and the George IV Bridge, its cramped and towering tenements were filled to capacity, and a warren of cellars below reeked of filth and poverty. The great fire of Edinburgh had cleansed the upper slopes of the rickety wooden 'lands', but down in the lowest levels of the Cowgate valley, the underground city still thrived.

The Cowgate has been the birthplace of more than one famous man. Walter Scott, the novelist, was born there, when the Cowgate was a bit more respectable. James Connelly, the famous Irish leader, was born there, when the worst excesses of the Cowgate were past. But, in 1830, at the height of its notoriety, a child was born into abject poverty

Old houses in the Cowgate

in the darkness of the Cowgate cellars. A child who, while never achieving the fame he deserved, became as notorious as the place where he was born. His name was William Topaz McGonagall.

McGonagall is usually associated with the city of Dundee, but it was in the Cowgate that he grew up and in the Cowgate he eventually died. McGonagall's father was one of the many poor Irish immigrants who had come to the capital of Scotland in the early part of the nineteenth century – an influx so great that the population doubled in thirty years. He had left the green but unproductive fields of his native land hoping to make a better life for himself and his family. He didn't. He struggled to support them for some time in Ayr, then moved to Edinburgh where, after a number of fruitless years in the slums and cellars trying to provide for his wife and five children, he gave up and moved to Glasgow; then Orkney; then Dundee. As a result McGonagall grew up with very little schooling, but a great deal of tenacity – which he needed once he started writing poetry.

Most of William McGonagall's life was entirely uneventful. He lived in Dundee and worked long hours as a weaver for most of his life. Despite his lack of formal education, he loved classic literature, with a particular passion for Shakespeare. He wrote in his autobiography, *The Autobiography of Sir William Topaz McGonagall, Poet and Tragedian, Knight of the White Elephant of Burma* (titles he took very seriously, though they were all practical jokes played on him):

> The books I liked best were Shakespeare's penny plays, more especially Macbeth, Richard III, Hamlet and Othello; and I gave myself no rest until I obtained complete mastery over the above four characters.

According to the accounts of the time this 'mastery' of Shakespearean characters had to be seen to be believed and were almost as dreadful as his poetry recitals. Amazingly, McGonagall didn't write a poem until the age of fifty-two, when he received 'divine inspiration'. As he put it so eloquently in his autobiography:

> It was the year of 1877 and in the month of June, when the flowers were in full bloom. [Even then the poetry was creeping in.] Well, it being the holiday week in Dundee, I was sitting in my back-room in Paton's Lane, Dundee, lamenting to myself because I couldn't get to the Highlands on holiday to see the beautiful scenery when all of a sudden my body got inflamed, and instantly I was seized with a strong desire to write poetry, so strong, in fact, that in my imagination I thought I heard a voice crying in my ears – Write! Write!

And write he did. He gave up his weaving job and spent the rest of his life composing literary gems – 215 pieces in all, including a play. But it is for his poetry that William Topaz McGonagall will, quite rightly, be remembered. It is disjointed, doesn't scan, and goes off on many tangents at the drop of a hat. The rhyme is basic and pays no attention to the overall narrative. If McGonagall found two words he liked that rhymed, he would use them over and over again – often within the same poem. A perfect example of the awfulness he could achieve is encapsulated in the last verse of 'The Burns Statue':

> Fellow citizens, this statue seems most
>   beautiful to the eye,
> Which would cause Kings and Queens for
>   such a one to sigh,
> And make them feel envious while passing by
> In fear of not getting such a beautiful statue
>   after they die.

He was actually very popular in Dundee. Crowds would flock to hear his recitals and his interpretation of Shakespearean classics, but not to appreciate them. Rather, they would treat the whole thing as comic entertainment and quite frequently fire peas or launch tomatoes at the unfortunate bard.

McGonagall, though, was pretty much devoid of

humour and convinced of his own genius – a conviction which never wavered. His dedication to his art was quite astonishing. He desperately wanted the patronage of Queen Victoria and walked fifty miles on foot to try and convince her of this. When he reached the gates of Balmoral and tried to bluff his way in, he was told never to come back. He went to London, lured by forged invitations (McGonagall was the butt of countless practical jokes which he never seemed to see through, even after they had been revealed to him). He even travelled to New York, arriving with only eight shillings. Americans didn't like his poetry any more than the Scots or the English and he quickly came back.

McGonagall is an enigma. There are those who claim that he knew what a completely rotten poet he was all along and simply built up his buffoon-like character, actually encouraging jeers and jibes in order to keep his family out of the conditions into which he was born – the weaving industry in Dundee at that time was rapidly dying and plunging the struggling workers into even more poverty. Certainly, he was encouraged by some of the great philanthropists of the time, one of whom paid for his passage back from New York. And Lewes Spence tells of how McGonagall was able to 'discourse intelligently' on the likes of Shakespeare and Swinbourne.

In the end, though, his poetry is the deciding factor. Nobody, no matter how great their literary talent, could deliberately write such bad poetry. It takes a truly special kind of genius to write such awful poetry on so many levels, and still be entertaining.

There is a sad ending to McGonagall's story and it comes back, once again, to the underground city. McGonagall had a love/hate relationship with Dundee but eventually the hate side won:

> Welcome! Thrice welcome! To the year
>   1893,
> For it is the year I intend to leave
>   Dundee,
> Owing to the treatment I receive
> Which does my heart sadly grieve.
> Every morning when I go out
> The ignorant rabble they do shout
> 'There goes mad McGonagall'
> In derisive shouts as loud as they can
>   bawl,
> And lifts stones and snowballs, throws
>   them at me;
> And such actions are shameful to be
>   heard in the city of Dundee.
> And I'm ashamed, kind Christians to
>   confess,
> That from the magistrates I can get no
>   redress.
> Therefore I have made up my mind, in
>   the year of 1893,

To leave the Ancient city of Dundee,
Because the citizens and I cannot agree.
The reason why? – because they
        disrespect me,
Which makes me feel rather discontent.
Therefore to leave them I am bent;
And I will make my arrangements
        without delay,
And leave Dundee some early day.

The poem itself may be abysmal but, in a strange way, there is more pathos and honesty in it than most romantic poets of the time ever achieved.

Near the end of his life, McGonagall finally did move back to Edinburgh, where he was in vogue with the upper classes for a while as comic entertainment – they found him just as jaw-droppingly bad as Dundee had. But, eventually, he fell from grace. At the end of his life he found himself, to his horror, back in the cellars of the Cowgate. His poetry was prolific and covered every kind of event and location imaginable, including several about Edinburgh – but they never touch on the slums or the squalor where he was born and where finally he died.

It was William McGonagall's dearest wish (apart from becoming Poet Laureate) that he be buried in Poet's Corner in Westminster Abbey. Instead, he was buried in an unmarked grave in Greyfriars Churchyard, its location now forgotten.

The exact place of his birth is lost too. There isn't even a plaque to indicate the rough location. But then, Walter Scott doesn't have one either and he was once the most famous man in Europe.

McGonagall had the last laugh in a way. Everything he ever wrote has been published, and he is remembered by legions of loyal readers long after more famous contemporaries have faded from memory. Just as Shakespeare, his idol, is regarded as the greatest literary writer in history – McGonagall is without doubt, the worst and, as such, is equally deserving of his place in history.

Escape to the West

In Hunter Square, behind the Tron Church, there is a popular High Street pub where, some years ago, a very strange set of events occurred.

The owner of the bar was curious as to exactly what was under his establishment. He dug a hole in the lowest level of his bar, next to the toilets, to see if the ruins of Marlin's Wynd still existed below his property. He dropped, not into Marlin's Wynd, but into a tunnel – once part of old Edinburgh's poultry market. Exploring this tunnel he was confronted by a wall so, in the spirit of an adventure already begun, he demolished it – and fell through a shop roof in a neighbouring, but less-elevated street.

The publican apologised to the startled shopkeeper and sealed the tunnel again. But he would find himself down there one more time, in the oddest of circumstances.

A few years later an East European rugby team – in Edinburgh for a match against Scotland – ended up drinking in the very same High Street bar. One foreign player, enjoying the hospitality (and almost certainly the whisky), let it be known that he longed to defect, but this seemed impossible as his team were constantly surrounded by security guards.

With a knowing wink, the owner led the puzzled player downstairs to the toilets. Not knowing quite what to expect the would-be defector was astonished, as well as greatly relieved, when the publican revealed the perfect escape route – the hidden tunnel. The two men dropped into it and emerged undetected at the other end from where the rugby player made his getaway.

He successfully defected and lives in Britain to this day.

Nowadays the hidden passage is completely sealed up. This is not to prevent any more defections – more likely it is to stop thieves travelling in the opposite direction and helping themselves to the contents of the bar.

Encounter under
the North Bridge

Buttressing the North Bridge is a huge thirteen-storey building – the old headquarters of *The Scotsman* newspaper and the Edinburgh *Evening News*. Anyone living in Edinburgh will be familiar with the long, sinister (and rather odorous) flight of stairs which starts at the junction of the south end of the bridge and the building, winds down into the darkness and finally emerges at Waverley Station.

The building utilises several of the adjoining bridge vaults – many containing printing presses – some long unused. Not surprisingly, these rooms, as with so many sections of the bridge vaults, have quite a reputation for being haunted.

On one occasion a page-make-up artist working for the *Evening News* found himself in one of the

The North Bridge and the Bank of Scotland, from a
drawing by Sir John Carr published in 1809

little-used basement areas of the massive building – a section where the old, unused printing presses still stood. He was walking past a door, when it suddenly occurred to him that he couldn't remember ever seeing a door there before. Being in the newspaper business, he was naturally curious. He opened the mysterious portal and found a dimly lit flight of stairs. Showing the kind of bravado that have won reporters the Pulitzer Prize, he descended.

Below him was a corridor and he observed a man striding purposefully along it. The stranger wore brown trousers and a brown jersey and was wearing a blue apron tied at the back. He appeared to be hard at work and was carrying a large wooden tray filled with some kind of metal boxes. He looked like a printer and didn't act or appear to be out of place in the slightest – apart from his rather old-fashioned garb. Then the page-maker noticed something very odd, and the hairs stood up on the back of his neck. The printer wasn't making any noise. None at all. There should have been the sound of his footfalls, the rustle of his apron against his legs, the clink of metal upon metal in his tray. Instead there was only a terrifying silence. The page-maker suddenly felt an overpowering feeling of unease and shot back up the stairs. Moments later his work colleagues were startled by the sight of their wild-eyed co-worker bursting back into the office. His face was white, his hair was drenched in sweat and he was mumbling something about taking early retirement.

The page-maker did go down to the basements again, this time with three colleagues for moral and physical support. There was only one door there and it was locked. Yet the mysterious printer had appeared far too quickly in the corridor to have unlocked then locked the door again. Besides, the pagemaker hadn't heard any rattling of locks or keys. There was only one conclusion he could come to. He had seen a ghost.

This is not the only ghost to haunt the North Bridge. A security guard in the *Evening News* building found himself encountering an employee who had died in 1990. The building is also haunted by a particularly annoying ghost – a blonde woman who always dresses in black and seems to be particularly fond of the information counter. She will walk towards the staff entrance door as if she is about to politely open it for one of her colleagues, then suddenly duck under the counter and disappear. She is also fond of approaching the counter from the front, as if she is a customer, then disappearing into thin air when anyone tries to help her. Obviously some ghosts will do anything just to get their name in print.

The Foreman

A group of workmen were contracted to renovate some underground vaults below the South Bridge. In one chamber, two workers had been given the task of demolishing a wall. With typical enthusiasm they chipped away a couple of bricks, then went outside for a cigarette.

After their break they reluctantly crept back through the gloomy tunnels, stopping at every imagined movement or sound. Suddenly, their thermos flasks dropped from shaking, nicotine-stained fingers as they realised that one sound wasn't imaginary. Approaching the vault they had been working on, both men could hear a sinister moaning issuing forth from the darkness. They crept slowly forward, wide-eyed, until a blood-curdling wail sent them scrambling back through the passages and into the sunlight.

The *Scotsman* office

Tackling ghosts definitely wasn't in their job description, so they went and fetched the foreman.

Tam the foreman was a large, broad fellow. He didn't believe in ghosts and – if he did – he wasn't scared of them. He laced up his steel-toed boots, stuck his hard hat at a jaunty angle and marched into the vaults to give this supernatural tool-downer a good kick in the rear.

But the tunnel seemed more foreboding with each step and the dark vault doors began to look like gaping, open tombs. Tam's march slowed to a shuffle as his imagination conjured up all sorts of toothy, bug-eyed apparitions lurking inside the black chambers.

Then he heard it. A low inhuman moan drifting down the tunnel from a vault at the top. A moan that made his flesh crawl. Then another moan. And another.

The terrified foreman had two choices. He could carry on and face the hideous creature responsible for these hair-raising wails . . . or he could run back to safety and have the other workmen laugh and call him a big girl's blouse for the rest of his life.

He carried on.

As he inched into the pitch-black vault the groaning rose to a deafening pitch – yet Tam's wildly swinging flashlight revealed there was nobody in the chamber. With a gasp, the terrified foreman realised that another shaft of light pierced the blackness – it was shining straight out of the opposite wall. The terrible groans were coming from there. Mesmerised with horror Tam slowly crossed the vault to the source of light and noise.

It was an opening, the one his workmen had made. In the wrong wall.

Tam peered through and saw exactly what was responsible for the noise.

His men had knocked a hole through to a massage parlour.

The Witches' Temple

In 1996 a small coven of Scottish witches were given permission to use an underground vault as a place of worship. On entering chambers underneath the South Bridge the coven leader, George Cameron, knew immediately where his pagan temple should be located. One vault in particular, he claimed, had more 'psychic energy' than the rest and was perfect for his purposes.

By a happy coincidence it was also the driest and warmest vault. This was soon to change.

The coven built a pagan temple in the vault. A witches' circle of stone was constructed and 'powered up' and protective spells were cast over the religious artefacts inside. In one corner George placed a large upright mirror which was required for certain ceremonies. It was a decoration he was to bitterly regret.

At first everything seemed normal – at least as normal as a pagan temple can be. The coven had the use of the vault for rituals late at night. (They were white witches, so no devil worship or human sacrifice was going on.) During the day visitors to the underground chambers were allowed to look into the witches' chamber, if they wished, and marvel at the strange objects inside. Then things began to go wrong.

The coven leader himself was the first to be alarmed. He had always insisted he could feel long-dead spirits wandering through the vaults – but they had always been friendly. Now he sensed a new and very different presence. Something evil, he insisted, had invaded the vaults. To challenge this entity he prepared to spend the night alone in his temple. This was an act of quite astonishing bravery – as anyone who has ever seen these black, gloomy chambers will readily testify.

Just after midnight, George heard something crawling through the blackness near the mirror. Too afraid to switch on his flashlight, he chanted incantations designed to keep the unseen intruder at bay. It worked. The entity would not cross into the stone circle where George sheltered. The white witch had won the first battle. But this was only the beginning of George's troubles.

On three occasions, visitors to the pagan temple were terrified as temperatures in the vault dropped to a level painful to the flesh and condensation rose from their hands and faces. Others complained that the mirror at the back of George's vault made them 'uneasy'. Some claimed to have seen the reflection of a 'large, white figure' on its surface and two women even shouted that 'something white' had stepped out of the mirror and back again.

One visitor, a recognised psychic, put it simply.

'That isn't a mirror,' he said, pointing to the offending object. 'It's a door. It's a door and it's letting in evil.'

George, who had stayed silent about these sightings, reluctantly agreed. Instead of putting in a free-standing mirror in the vault, as ceremonies required, he had used a mirror stuck on the front of a wardrobe door. The psychic had been right.

George was not the type to give in to demons, so he began casting protective spells over the mirror. By this time, however, the temple was in near ruins. Though the roof and three vault walls were perfectly dry, the wall nearest the mirror was soaking wet and clumps of yellow oxidisation had formed on the surface. The vault had been dry for 150 years, but now the mirror sat in an expanding pool of dark and foul-smelling water. On 18 October 1996, the temple was moved to another vault.

George, fascinated by the apparent power of the mirror, insisted that it go too. As soon as it was moved, the old vault began to dry up. Within weeks all the water was gone.

The new pagan temple fared no better than the

old one. On a number of occasions the mirror was found face down but unbroken on the stone floor – even though the new vault was locked. In the vault next door, a tour party experienced a sudden temperature drop. Two children, aged three and four, began to cry and point at a seemingly empty corner of the vault. They insisted that the 'man from the mirror' was frightening them.

There is an interesting footnote to this story. The mirror was found cracked one morning, even though it had been undamaged when the vaults were locked the night before. George asked one of his friends to remove it and throw it away. The unfortunate man was hit by a car a few days later.

Trapped!

During the eighteenth century a jeweller's shop in the Old Town used underground vaults as a store-room – the vault door (complete with an eighteenth-century wooden lock) still bears the jeweller's name: James Henderson. This underground storeroom has another unusual feature: a light shaft runs from the vault up to the street and allows a little sunlight to filter down.

The mouth of the shaft emerges at ground level on Niddry Street, where it is boarded over – presumably to prevent adventurous children sliding into the darkness and never being heard of again. Since the aperture is small and ankle-high, nobody pays much attention to it – but sometimes the board blocking the shaft is forced off. Whether this is the work of vandals trying to get in or demonic forces trying to get out is open to debate, but the aperture is sealed again as soon as anyone notices.

On one rare occasion, however, the board was missing and two passing Canadian backpackers spotted the exposed shaft. They had heard of the underground city and correctly guessed it was a way into the lowest level of the South Bridge vaults. Running to their nearby hostel, the pair returned with a couple of flashlights, ready to venture into the unknown. Getting into the shaft was a bit of a squeeze but this pair had explored half the globe – they weren't going to let a few doughnuts too many stop them. They wriggled down the shaft and emerged in the black interior of the jeweller's storeroom. Through the open door their flashlights revealed crumbling vaults stretching in every direction. Hushed and nervous they began to walk through the chambers, their trepidation turning to awe as more and more vaults were revealed. It was about then that one of the flashlights went out.

The Canadians were adventurous but not fool-hardy – they decided to return to the surface. A few feet further on the second flashlight extinguished.

The pair had turned several corners and could no longer see the light shining down the shaft into the storeroom – in fact they couldn't see their hands in front of their faces.

But backpackers are a stubborn bunch and natural explorers to boot. The Canadians were confident about retracing their steps. They set off in the direction they had come, one deliberate step at a time, feeling their way blindly along the wall. Two hours later they were still lost.

By this time their nerves were shredded and their composure had utterly vanished – along with their sense of direction. They had lost count of the number of turns they had taken – or the times they had stumbled and fallen – and their throats were raw from shouting for help.

Finally, as complete insanity was setting in, one of the backpackers felt wood under his fingers – the storeroom door. He pushed it open . . . and found only more blackness.

The shaft of light had gone. Someone had replaced the covering board while the explorers were inside. Despite the condition of their throats this prompted the Canadians into another round of maniacal screaming. This time, however, they were just below the street and a passer-by heard their cries. He prised away the board and the backpackers scrambled wildly up the shaft, collapsed on to the pavement and lay gasping for air.

Both were shaken and grimy and probably left with a lifelong fear of enclosed spaces – but that was not all. When they saw each other's face they almost fainted. Though the backpackers had felt nothing, their foreheads and cheeks were a mass of scratches – all evenly spaced.

Exactly the marks claws would make.

The Ghosts of
Whistle Binkies

The number of ghost stories attached to the Old Town are legion – and the streets and vaults in the South Bridge area have more than their fair share. The bridge itself is famous as a 'jinxed' structure – a reputation going back to the day it was built. The local dignitary chosen for the ceremonial first crossing died days before the opening. She ended up fulfilling her duty in a coffin. A hearse was the first vehicle ever to cross the South Bridge.

One of the local ghosts has been nicknamed the 'Imp' as he seems to be a mischievous sort. He moves objects around in the cellars of pubs and shops under the Bridge and, oddly enough, haunts the kitchen and laundry of a backpackers' hostel in nearby Blackfriar's Wynd. In one South Bridge shop he would rearrange earrings and other shiny objects once the staff had gone home – mind you, it's hard to be scared of a ghost that likes earrings.

When the South Bridge vaults were opened for public tours in 1994, the Imp moved in. For several months there were regular incidences of flashlights flickering and failing during the underground tours. The torches would dim then brighten, work in some vaults and not in others. On one tour every single flashlight went out and visitors had to reload the failed torches with their camera batteries – not an easy task to perform in pitch-blackness, especially while surrounded by screaming companions.

For a short while another ghost – the 'Watcher' – was also a regular in the vaults. He was dressed in seventeenth-century garb and was tall with long hair. On one memorable occasion a tour party mistook him for a costumed guide and followed him into a chamber which turned out to be empty.

One site, in particular, seems to be plagued by these two spectres – Whistle Binkies Bar – a public house built into the converted chambers below the South Bridge. Since opening in 1994 it has become a regular haunt of these two ghosts.

The Watcher was sighted while the pub was still under construction. Walking into the unfinished building, the bar designer found a woman in a long, heavy dress standing at the cellar door with her back to the room. Ignoring the designer's questions, the woman walked down the stairs and into the cellar. When he ran after her, he found the cellar empty.

The astonished man drew a picture of what he had seen and showed it to a local historian. The historian pointed out that this 'woman' was wearing a seventeenth-century gentleman's coat – not a dress. The designer, seeing long hair, had assumed what he was looking at was female. In fact, he had come across the Watcher.

The historian was curious. He wanted to ascertain that this supernatural sighting was authentic and not the result of another kind of spirit altogether. He inquired casually as to the colour of the ghost's coat – a trick question of sorts. In seventeenth-century Edinburgh, gentlemen's coats of the type in the picture were required by law to be a certain colour – a fact very few people would know. The designer gave the correct two colours. He really had seen a ghost.

The Watcher has been sighted several times in the bar, though he never attempts to buy a drink. Stranger still, nobody has ever been able to describe his face – even the designer's sketch shows him from the back.

Perhaps he has a very forgettable face; perhaps he was the victim of one of the Old Town fires; perhaps he was infected by Edinburgh's plague of 1645; perhaps rats ate his face before he died.

The Imp also seems to be a regular in Whistle Binkies – and full of annoying tricks. According to staff he likes to stop the pub clock at 4.15 in the morning. On one particular evening, after the customers had been thrown out, two of the barmaids were washing and putting away glasses. One girl had saved an orange from her break and was going to eat it once her work was finished. As she was about to peel it she noticed a couple of glasses left on the windowsill of the pub. She set the fruit on the bar, trudged wearily to the window and retrieved the glasses. Turning back to the bar she let out a scream. In the few seconds her back was turned, the Imp had obligingly chopped and peeled the orange for her.

The Imp is hardly the scariest ghost in Edinburgh – but he does have his moments. One barmaid, Kate Sinclair, was alone in the pub stocking the bar before opening time. She went down to the cellar to bring up some wine – not a task she enjoyed as the cellar scared her. She found a case of wine at the back of the furthest small, low-ceilinged vault, heaved it into her arms and staggered towards the stairs. Still carrying the heavy case, she tried to kick the cellar door open with her foot. It wouldn't budge. She put the case down and pushed. The door didn't move. She pulled instead – just in case she had forgotten which way the door opened. It stayed put. She knew the door couldn't lock itself but she tried the key anyway. As she suspected, it wasn't locked, it must be stuck. She pushed harder but the door wouldn't give an inch.

Kate Sinclair was trapped in a tiny cellar, on her own, in a bar she knew was haunted. She shoulder-charged the door. She hit it with a chair. She screamed for help. Nothing.

Eventually she sat down on the chair with a bottle of vodka, hung her head and began to cry. As she sobbed, there was a creaking at the other end of the room. Kate looked up. The door swung open and she was able to leave.

The South Bridge chambers opened to visitors around the same time as Whistle Binkies, so it is not strange that the Imp and the Watcher were reported down there too. But not for long.

From around June 1995 a third presence made itself felt in the vaults. The Imp and the Watcher were either playful or totally indifferent to visitors, but they never harmed anyone. This new entity was different.

Local residents felt that development work under the bridge, the building of two underground nightclubs and the opening of vaults to tour parties had disturbed something. And this 'something' wasn't pleased – in fact, it was mad as hell. The new entity was christened the 'South Bridge Entity' – and it wasn't just people that it frightened.

After its arrival, the Imp and the Watcher were not sighted in the underground city again.

The South Bridge Entity

The South Bridge Entity is a less-than-pleasant addition to underground city lore, and there have been a number of theories as to just what this super-natural creature might be. Most believe it is the ghost of Bloody McKenzie, a judge in the pay of King Charles I and the ruthless persecutor of a religious group known as Covenanters. His house was right opposite the site of the South Bridge. Others claim it is the ghost responsible for the many fires that have plagued the central section of the Royal Mile. A more scientific theory suggests that the Entity is a particularly lively poltergeist – an idea backed by the fact that it is felt rather than seen and is most active when children are in the vaults. The claim that the Entity and Bloody McKenzie's ghost are one and the same is borne out by similar sightings – which are even more disturbing and prolific – in Greyfriars Churchyard further up the Royal Mile. The churchyard just happens to be the burial place of Bloody McKenzie and the Covenanters he executed.

Whatever its true identity, any visitors who have encountered the Entity in its underground lair have no doubts about its character. It is evil.

The Entity's presence was heralded by the strange phenomenon known as 'cold spots'. In June 1995, two Australian visitors to the vaults, Susan Harvey and Susan Douglas, experienced the first cold spots in the underground chambers. Standing in a vault doorway the girls suddenly felt abnormally chilled. As they tried to move further into the vault, one of the girls, overcome by a powerful nausea, staggered and almost fell. The other put out an arm to steady her friend then let out a scream and backed hurriedly into the vault. Nothing sinister was actually visible, but one or two braver visitors stretched their arms into the doorway to feel what the girl had touched.

Though the vault itself and the passage outside were temperate, the air in that one space was so cold it was painful on their flesh.

This occurrence set a pattern. In December 1995, a Polish student named Maja Szeresewska was standing in a vault corner and began shivering and then fainted. On the wall behind the girl, a patch of stonework three feet long was cold as ice. Again the temperature on the rest of the wall was normal.

stop at 4.15 in the morning.

➤ A member of staff runs from the cellar after hearing shuffling noises all around her.

➤ Resurgence of the hammering noises that used to plague band practice rooms under the South Bridge. At one point, frightened staff run into the street.

➤ Workmen sight the Watcher in underground vaults.

April 1995

➤ The first instances of flashlights flickering and failing in South Bridge vaults. These incidents occur regularly for the next three months then they tail off.

➤ A psychic on a tour refuses to enter one large vault – the Haunted Vault – claiming that it is possessed.

➤ Twelve flashlights fail on the same tour and have to be reloaded using visitors' camera batteries.

May 1995

➤ The Watcher is sighted by a tour party of sixteen people.

➤ Flashlights begin to get rapidly brighter and dimmer in the Haunted Vault even when placed on their own on the ground.

➤ First instance of strange lights in vaults. These are seen frequently for the next two months then suddenly stop again. Most common are a small green glow inside one vault, a white light shining from a vault doorway and a cross-shaped light in a passageway. All the lights fade away when approached.

➤ Staff in Whistle Binkies begin to complain repeatedly of 'things moving around' in the cellar.

➤ Staff member cleaning the Haunted Vault sees 'something crouching' next to him.

June 1995

➤ A light that constantly changes shape is seen in an underground passage by twenty to twenty-five students.

➤ A large tour party spots a 'cross-shaped light' in an underground passage. It changes shape as they watch. Photographs, when developed, reveal nothing at all.

➤ An eleven-year-old Scots girl sights a bright luminescence at the end of a passageway but it fades as she walks towards it.

➤ The same girl returns two days later. So does the luminescence.

➤ Two Australian visitors experience the first cold spot. Cold spots occur sporadically from this point on. At the same time a green glow is sighted at the top of the passage where they are standing.

July 1995

➤ Spectral light appears in passageway. Only half the visitors there can see it – and everyone describes it in a different way.

➤ The eleven-year-old girl returns for the last time. Luminescence appears in tunnel again. As the girl passes one of the vault doorways the small green glow is also sighted. Though this particular incandescence has never moved, it retreats further into the vault as she looks at it. Neither of these particular lights is seen again.

➤ Six flashlights dim in an underground tunnel only to return to full power when they are moved to an adjacent vault.

➤ A visitor becomes frantic in the Haunted

Vault, shouting that something is trying to grab hold of her.

➤ American backpacker has contents of his rucksack pulled out and smashed on the ground. Nobody is standing near him.

August 1995

➤ An eleven-year-old boy emerges from vault tour with one arm covered in scratches. He claims that something hit him from the darkness above.

➤ A small dog goes into frenzy when owner tries to carry him into the Haunted Vault.

September 1995

➤ A voice snarls at staff member in Haunted Vault.

November 1995

➤ Workmen in the vaults claim that someone keeps switching off their radio – though it is in full view and nobody is standing near it.

December 1995

➤ A visitor collapses in the vault and a cold spot is found behind her.

January 1996

➤ A visiting psychic announces a 'friendly presence' in one particular vault.

February 1996

➤ A psychic announces that there is a 'malicious' presence in the Haunted Vault and refuses to go further into the underground city. He draws a psychic map of what he has seen.

➤ A coven of white witches is given permission to build a pagan temple in one of the South Bridge vaults and to worship there. They choose this site because they believe the hidden chambers have 'psychic energy on an incredible scale'.

➤ The coven leader spends the night in a witches' circle in the vaults. He claims that 'something evil' tried to enter the circle all night.

March 1996

➤ A visitor collapses in the Haunted Vault. A cold spot is found right behind her.

➤ A visiting psychic claims that the mirror in the pagan temple is acting as a 'portal' for a demonic force. This statement seems to be backed by other visitors claiming to have any kind of psychic ability. They all state that the mirror is 'evil' in some way.

April 1996

➤ A tourist collapses in the Haunted Vault. A cold spot is found behind her.

➤ A visitor to the vaults claims that an invisible entity 'grabbed' at her head.

➤ A tour party spots the outline of a man moving along the corridor outside the Haunted Vault.

➤ Four women in the Haunted Vault are knocked away from the wall on which they are leaning by an invisible entity.

➤ A visitor collapses in the Haunted Vault. A cold spot is found behind her.

➤ The temperature in the pagan temple suddenly drops to a degree that is painful on the flesh and condensation rises from the faces and hands of visitors.

➤ There is an identical occurrence in a small chamber behind the Haunted Vault. Condensation rises from the back of a tour guide as he stands at the entrance of the chamber.

➤ A visitor from another pagan coven announces that 'something is terribly wrong' around the witches' circle in the pagan temple.

➤ A large wooden barrier in the Haunted Vault inexplicably tips over and crashes to the ground – narrowly missing a group of visitors.

May 1996

➤ Visitors see an old woman walking across a vault. The vault turns out to be empty.

June 1996

➤ A visitor complains of something 'freezing cold' pushing against her head.

➤ A business manager breaks down in the vault, sobbing that 'something very cold' is pressing against her head.

➤ The regional co-ordinator for the

Association for the Scientific Study of Anomalous Phenomena – a national group of psychic investigators – visits the underground city. He begins an investigation into the South Bridge vaults.

July 1996

➤ Something pushes through a group of visitors. Though they feel it, the people in the vault cannot see what is brushing past them.

July–August 1996

➤ Visitors and tour guides see a 'white figure' reflected in the upright mirror in the pagan temple. This happens several times. Visitors also complain that the mirror makes them feel uneasy.

August 1996

➤ Water begins to leak through one section of the vault wall in the pagan temple – right beside the mirror. The rest of the chamber remains dry.

September 1996

➤ A ten-year-old boy collapses in a vault and has to be carried outside. His statement is that something cold was holding his head. His mother complains of the same sensation.

➤ A mother and daughter believe they are holding hands in the darkness. In fact neither of them is standing near each other – or anybody else for that matter.

➤ Visitors leaving the Haunted Vault retreat back as something runs up the corridor outside and stops at the vault door. Though breathing and footsteps can plainly be heard, the passage outside is empty.

October 1996

➤ The pagan temple is now in ruins and the mirror sits in a pond of foul-smelling water. On 18 October the temple is moved to another vault. The mirror goes with it.

➤ Scottish Television films the strange flooding in the old pagan temple. Now that the mirror has gone, the vault begins to dry up.

➤ The Watcher appears twice in Whistle Binkies after an absence of more than a year.

November 1996

➤ Tour guides begin to complain that they are being hit or jostled in the Haunted Vault by something they cannot see.

➤ Three- and four-year-old children in the vault begin to cry at the appearance of the 'man from the mirror'. The rest of the visitors cannot see anything.

➤ A visiting psychic draws another map of the entities he has seen in the vaults.

December 1996

➤ The mirror, now in the new pagan temple, is twice found face down but unbroken on the vault floor.

➤ A woman in the Haunted Vault complains that her skin is 'burning'. The sensation stops as soon as she exits the vault.

January 1997

➤ Sightings grow progressively less frequent. From 1997 to 1999 there are only a handful.

June 1998–January 1999

➤ Occasional tours begin in Greyfriars Churchyard. On each tour, visitors complain of intense cold near Bloody McKenzie's tomb. On one tour a young boy appears to be catapulted backwards into a gravestone. The tours are abandoned.

March 1999

➤ A group of underground tour guides, perhaps missing their old adversary, begin the first regular tour of Greyfriars. On the very first one, the tour guide is knocked to the ground in front of several witnesses who complain of suddenly being freezing cold.

These tours continue.

Bibliography

Arnot, Hugo (1779), *The History of Edinburgh*, West Port Books

Bell, George MD, *Blackfriar's Wynd Analysed*

Birrell, J.F. (1980), *An Edinburgh Alphabet*, The Mercat Press

Books of the Old Edinburgh Club (Vols I to present)

Daiches, David (1978), *Edinburgh*, Hamish Hamilton

Gillon, J.K. (1990), *Eccentric Edinburgh*, Moubray House Publishing

Grant, James (1884–1887), *Old and New Edinburgh Vols I–III*

Grierson, Flora, *Haunting Edinburgh*

Hanney, R.K. and Watson, G., *The Building of Parliament House*

McGonagall, William Topaz, *Last Poetic Gems*,

David Winter & Son Ltd

Macleod, W. and Wood, M. (ed.), *Protocol Books of John Fowler (1501–28)*, Scottish Record Society

Maitland, W. (1753), *A History of Edinburgh*

Martin, G.H. and McIntyre, S., *A Bibliography of British and Irish Municipal History*

Minto, C.S. (1975), *Edinburgh, Past and Present*, Oxford Illustrated Press

Phillips, David (1971), *No Poets' Corner in the Abbey*, David Winter & Son Ltd

Sinclair, George, *Satan's Invisible World*

Smith, J.C. (1978), *Historic South Edinburgh*, Charles Skilton Ltd

Smith, Mrs J. Stewart (1924), *Historic Stories of Bygone Edinburgh*, T&A Constable Ltd

Stevenson, Robert Louis (1878), *Picturesque Old Edinburgh*, Albyn Press Ltd

Turnbull, Michael T.R.B. (1991), *The Edinburgh Book of Quotations*, B&W Publishings

Turnbull, Michael (1987), *Edinburgh Portraits*, John Donald Publishers Ltd

Wood, Margaret (1929), *Edinburgh 1329–1929 & Survey of the Development of Edinburgh*

The *Daily Record*, the *Edinburgh Evening News* and *The Scotsman* newspaper

ALSO AVAILABLE FROM MAINSTREAM

**GHOSTLY TALES &
SINISTER STORIES
OF OLD
EDINBURGH**

£6.99
ISBN 9781851584567

Over a hundred gripping tales – of murder and mystery, ghosts and ghouls, body-snatching and witch-burning – reveal the darker side of genteel Edinburgh's history.

Ghostly Tales and Sinister Stories of Old Edinburgh is a highly readable collection, fully illustrated throughout and compiled by the three historians who operate Mercat Tours. Since 1984, thousands of visitors have enjoyed their nightly rounds of the closes and wynds of Edinburgh's Old Town. Now you can read of the macabre exploits of Edinburgh's infamous villains – Deacon Brodie, Burke and Hare, Major Weir, Agnes Fynnie and a host of others – which bring this ancient city intriguingly to life.

THE GHOST THAT HAUNTED ITSELF

£6.99
ISBN 9781840184822

Greyfriar's Cemetery in Edinburgh has a centuries old reputation for being haunted. Its gruesome history includes use as a mass prison, headstone removal, witchcraft, bodysnatching, desecration, corpse dumping and live burial.

But in 1998, something new and inexplicable began occurring in the graveyard. Visitors encountered 'cold spots', strange smells and banging noises. They found themselves overcome by nausea, or cut and bruised by something they could not see.

Over the space of two years, twenty-four people were knocked unconscious. Homes next to the graveyard wall became plagued by crockery smashing, objects moving and unidentified laughter Witnesses to these attacks ran into the hundreds. There were two exorcisms of the area. Both failed.

The section of Greyfriars where the attacks occurred is now chained shut. The entity responsible has been named the 'McKenzie Poltergeist'. It has become one of the best-documented and most conclusive paranormal cases in history.

The Poltergeist is still growing stronger. This is its story.